The German Kitchen

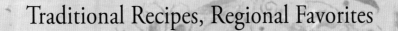

Traditional Recipes, Regional Favorites

The German Kitchen

Christopher and Catherine Knuth

Interlink Books

An imprint of Interlink Publishing Group, Inc.
Northampton, Massachusetts

To all who love and appreciate
good German food—enjoy.

CONTENTS

Introduction   8

Soups   14

Seafood   38

Meat, Game, & Poultry   62

Vegetables   124

Dressings & Sauces   153

Desserts   167

Acknowledgements   187

Index of Recipes   188

Introduction

My parents returned to Germany after a twelve-year absence, when I was three. We settled in Blankenese, a picturesque and somewhat genteel town on the outskirts of Hamburg, on the Elbe river. It has a long history as a fishing village and it was there that I spent my childhood and early adulthood. Growing up, there was always plenty to do: from fishing and sailing on the Elbe River, to hiking and bike riding with friends in the nearby forest, where we would often try to feed the wild pigs!

Blankenese's and Hamburg's culinary specialties are various types of fish, crab, herring. and eel, usually seasoned with numerous spices, in particular paprika, cayenne, cumin, and bay leaves. However, game, such as deer and wild pig, are also popular, as well as schnitzel—one of Germany's most famous food exports. Growing up near the sea within a close-knit farming community, my interest in produce and cooking was a natural progression. But first and foremost, I was inspired by my mother, who always took the time to cook hearty, seasonal meals for my brother and I. Sundays were a day of baking at our house in Blankenese. My mother would make my favorite cakes like *Rotweinkuchen* (Red Wine Cake) and *Schokoladenkuchen* (Chocolate Cake). We often had so much food left over we'd invite the neighbors in and it would always become quite the party. It was also during our baking Sundays that my mother would tell me about her memories of her time overseas, of the wonderful ingredients she found there and what was, at the time, a burgeoning wine industry.

The inspiration closest to my heart is my brother. He was a trained chef when he was killed in a tragic accident at the age of 21, so when thinking about what I wanted to do, I felt compelled to follow in his footsteps. And in this way, we remained close, by sharing our mutual love for cooking and fresh, seasonal ingredients.

Like most chefs, I'm classically trained. My chef apprenticeship was completed at Restaurant Mignon in Blankenese. But the time I enjoyed the most was assisting my brother's friend's family run their small guesthouse in the Black Forest. Long before the terms "kitchen garden" and "foraging" entered common parlance, we grew all our own produce in the garden at the house, and I'd often spend time in the forest to see what herbs, berries, and nuts we could pick and use.

Although I now live in a different country, I really enjoy drawing upon my German heritage and upbringing to cook the sort of food I came to love in Blankenese, this small, dreamy town, west of Hamburg. Many famous cities to the south of Hamburg, such as Munich, or to the east, such as Berlin, are landlocked and their cuisine is quite different, with far less emphasis on seafood. The one unifying factor, however, in all the various regions of Germany, is beer. Every German loves a good beer and most regions in Germany have a local brewery!

Perhaps the link to the sea brought me eventually to settle in a beautiful beachside suburb with my family. My wife and I own a small, authentic German restuarant called Das Kaffeehaus. It is here that we share with the local community, the delight of German food cooked with love and from the heart.

Christopher Knuth

Soups

An aromatic, deep green soup — truly satisfying.

RAHMSPINATSUPPE

Cream of Spinach Soup

Remove stems from the spinach leaves and bring the salted water to boil in a large pan. Add the spinach and cook for five to six minutes. Strain and reserve the liquid. Blend the spinach in a food processor or blender until puréed.

In a large pan, sauté the onions in the butter until pale golden brown. Remove from the heat and sprinkle in the flour, then return to the heat and a cook for another one to two minutes.

Stir in the liquid you reserved from the spinach and once it is all incorporated into the soup, bring it back to a boil. Cook until the texture is thick, then stir in the spinach purée and cream.

Adjust the seasoning to your liking and serve the soup in bowls. Garnish with the eggs and crumbled bacon pieces.

1¼lb (570g) fresh young spinach,
well washed
5 cups salted water
2 onions, finely chopped
2 tablespoons butter
3 tablespoons all-purpose flour
1 cup heavy whipping cream
salt and pepper
2 hard-boiled eggs, sliced
2 strips crumbled bacon

This is a terrific soup. It's quite refreshing and makes the perfect appetizer or light lunch.

GURKEN-JOGHURT-SUPPE MIT PINIENKERNE

Cucumber and Yogurt Soup *with Pine Nuts*

Peel the cucumber, dice the flesh into small bite-size pieces, and set aside.

Crush the garlic, pine nuts, salt, and pepper thoroughly using a mortar and pestle. Transfer the mixture into a large bowl and beat in the yogurt and diced cucumber. Add the water along with the lemon juice to taste.

To serve, pour the soup into bowls, scatter over a few pine nuts, drizzle with olive oil, and garnish with some fresh dill.

1 large cucumber

4 garlic cloves

¾ cup pine nuts

½ teaspoon salt

pepper, to taste

1⅔ cups (400ml) plain yogurt

½ cup (120ml) cold water

1–2 teaspoons lemon juice

½ cup pine nuts

1 teaspoon olive oil

dill

*A quick meal for one, or a nourishing family dish for
all times of the year.*

KÜRBISSUPPE MIT KORIANDER

SERVES 6

Curried Sweet Potato, Coriander, and Pumpkin Soup

1 butternut squash, peeled and
seeded
2 large sweet potatoes
4¼ cups (1 liter) vegetable or
chicken stock
1 large onion
1 teaspoon ground coriander
1 teaspoon cumin
1 teaspoon garam masala
1 teaspoon turmeric
salt and pepper
cilantro leaves, to taste
plain yogurt or sour cream

Dice the squash and sweet potatoes. In a large pot, bring the stock to a boil, add the diced squash and potatoes, and cook until soft.

Dice the onion. In a frying pan, sauté the onion with the ground coriander, cumin, garam masala, and turmeric until soft. Add the onion mixture to the pot with the potatoes and purée well with a hand blender, then simmer on low heat. Add salt and pepper to taste.

Chop the cilantro and add liberally to the soup, retaining some for garnish. Serve in bowls with a dollop of plain yogurt or sour cream and a sprinkle of cilantro.

This is a chunky and rustic soup and can be enjoyed perfectly with a glass of red wine and some crusty bread. A Knuth family favorite, it is a beautifully sustaining soup to warm the belly.

GULASCHSUPPE

Goulash Soup

1 tablespoon olive oil

14oz (400g) beef chuck steak, trimmed and cubed

1 medium brown onion, chopped

1 medium carrot, peeled and chopped

2 garlic cloves, crushed

1 teaspoon sweet paprika

3½ cups beef stock

14oz (400g) can diced tomatoes

1lb (450g) floury potatoes (sebago or russet), peeled and cubed

pepper, to taste

sour cream

fresh chives

Heat the oil in a saucepan over medium-high heat. Cook the steak, stirring constantly, in two batches, for two to three minutes or until browned. Transfer to a bowl.

Add the onion and carrot to the pan. Cook, stirring, for five minutes or until softened. Add the garlic and paprika. Cook, stirring, for 30 seconds or until fragrant. Stir in the stock and tomato.

Return the steak to the pan and bring to a boil. Reduce the heat to low, then simmer, covered, for one hour or until the steak is tender. Add the potatoes and cook, partially covered, for 30 minutes or until slightly thickened. Season with pepper.

Ladle into bowls, dollop with sour cream, and sprinkle with chives, then serve.

A wonderfully hearty soup and a meal in itself.

SERVES 8

GRAUPENSUPPE

German Barley Soup

Heat the butter in a very large saucepan over medium-high heat. Add the onion and cook, stirring, until soft, about five minutes. Add the barley, and cook, stirring, until lightly toasted, about five minutes. Add the stock, potato, carrot, celeriac, leek, marjoram, sausages, and bacon, and cook, stirring occasionally, until sausages are tender, about 35 minutes.

Remove the sausages and bacon from the saucepan, and thinly slice the sausages. Discard the bacon.

Season the soup with the nutmeg, salt, and pepper.

To serve, ladle the soup into serving bowls and garnish with parsley and the sliced sausage.

6 tablespoons (90g) unsalted butter
1 medium onion, finely chopped
1 cup pearl barley
8½ cups (2 liters) vegetable stock
½ cup peeled, finely chopped russet
   potatos
½ cup peeled, finely chopped carrots
½ cup peeled, finely chopped celeriac
½ cup finely chopped leek
1 teaspoon dried marjoram
2 German sausages such as
   bockwurst or bratwurst
2oz (60g) piece bacon
freshly grated nutmeg, to taste
salt and freshly ground black
   pepper, to taste
⅓ cup flat-leaf parsley leaves, thinly
   sliced

This classic soup is so delicious. It is also quick and easy to prepare.

ERBSEN-SCHINKEN-SUPPE

Ham and Green Pea Soup

Place ham or bacon bones in a large pot and cover with cold water. Add the lentils, barley, and onion and simmer for one and a half hours.

Cook the peas and purée them. Remove the meat from the soup, pull the meat from the bone, and add it back into the soup. Add the potatoes and puréed green peas and thoroughly stir. Season with salt and pepper to taste and add the stock cube, if using. Simmer until the potatoes are soft.

Ladle into bowls and serve.

½lb (250g) ham or bacon on the bone

1 cup mixed lentils

½ cup barley

1 onion

2 cups frozen peas

2 potatoes, diced

salt and pepper, to taste

1 vegetable stock cube, optional

This very simple soup is comfort in a bowl.

SERVES 4

KARTOFFEL-LAUCH-SUPPE MIT THYMIAN

Leek, Potato, and Thyme Soup

Dry the potato cubes on a paper towel.

Melt the butter in a saucepan and gradually add the leek and thyme. Sauté until golden, glazed, and soft. This process generally takes about four to five minutes. Add the potato and enough water to cover the vegetables. Cover and cook on low heat for 30 minutes.

Pour in the milk, add salt and pepper, and allow to simmer for a further 30 minutes.

Serve garnished with cream.

1 lb (450g) potatoes, diced into 1 in (3 cm) cubes

8 tablespoons (120g) butter

2 lb (900g) leeks, washed and trimmed

1 large sprig of fresh thyme

1¼ cups (300ml) whole milk

salt and pepper

¼ cup (60ml) heavy whipping cream

A nourishing soup just perfect to warm up your winter's evening.

LINSENSUPPE MIT SPECK

SERVES 6

Lentil, Bacon, and Bockwurst Soup

1–2 teaspoons oil

1 onion, chopped

1 carrot, chopped

2 celery stalks, chopped

1 leek, chopped

1 parsnip, diced

14oz (400g) bacon, fat and rind removed

2 bay leaves

1 cup brown lentils

8 cups water

3 bockwurst, bratwurst, or kransky sausage

salt and pepper to taste

flat-leaf parsley, chopped

bread, to serve

Heat the oil in a large saucepan and sauté the onion for five minutes until soft. Add the carrot, celery, leek, parsnip, bacon, and bay leaves. Stir and gently sauté until golden brown.

Rinse the lentils thoroughly and add to the saucepan. Pour in the water, bring to a boil, turn down the heat, stir, and simmer for about 40 to 50 minutes.

Cut the sausage into chunky pieces. Add to the saucepan and simmer until tender.

Season with salt and pepper, garnish with parsley, and serve with a slice of sourdough or rye bread.

You won't find an easier and tastier soup than this. The barley and chicken taste so good together. My oma would make this for me when I was young and feeling unwell.

OMA'S HÜHNERSUPPE

SERVES 6

Grandma's Chicken Soup

1½lb (750g) chicken pieces
   (thighs, drumsticks, wings)
salt and pepper
1 leek, diced
1 celery stalk, diced
1 onion, chopped
1 garlic clove
1 stalk rosemary
8 cups water
7oz (200g) pearl barley
1 bay leaf
2 carrots, peeled and diced
½ cup cream, optional
garden herbs of your choice

Sauté the chicken in a large frying pan until golden brown. Remove from the pan and season.

Add the leek, celery, onion, garlic, and rosemary to the pan and gently cook, stirring, for approximately six minutes, until soft. Return the chicken pieces to the saucepan and pour in the water. Add the pearl barley, bay leaf, and carrots, then bring to a boil. Skim the surface and reduce to a simmer. Cook, partially covered, for one hour until the chicken and barley are tender.

Season and ladle into serving bowls and garnish with cream and fresh garden herbs.

A hearty classic, full of traditional German ingredients, this soup is as authentic as it is satisfying.

SAUERKRAUT UND FLEISCHKLÖSCHEN SUPPE

Sauerkraut and Meatball Soup

Mix together the beef and the egg then season and form into meatballs.

Sauté the onions in the oil until translucent, add the sugar, and continue to sauté until golden brown.

Add drained sauerkraut. Continue to sauté for a few minutes, then add the paprika.

Pour in the beef broth and add the meatballs. Bring to a boil then simmer, covered, for about 15 minutes.

Add the potatoes and carrots and continue simmering for about 10 more minutes until the potatoes are tender.

Season with salt and pepper, if needed.

1lb (500g) lean ground beef

1 egg

salt and pepper

2 small onions, diced

¼ cup (60ml) oil

2 tablespoons sugar

1¾lb (800g) canned sauerkraut, drained

1 tablespoon paprika

4 cups beef broth (or bouillon)

1lb (500g) potatoes, peeled and diced into 1in (3cm) pieces

2 or 3 carrots, peeled and diced into 1in (3cm) pieces

An unusual combination that tastes just delicious.
And that red—magic!

ROTE BETE SUPPE MIT WEISSKOHL

Cabbage and Beet Soup

Heat the oil in a large saucepan, add the onion and garlic, and cook gently for five minutes.

Mix in the beet, pour in the stock, and boil until tender. Place in a blender, blend with the cider vinegar, and return to the saucepan.

Scatter the cabbage over the soup but don't stir. Cover and boil gently for five minutes, until the cabbage is almost cooked but still crunchy.

Serve with chives arranged on the top.

⅓ cup (80ml) grapeseed oil
1 onion, finely chopped
1 garlic clove, finely chopped
1 lb (450g) raw baby beets, diced
4¼ cups (1 liter) vegetable stock
2 tablespoons cider vinegar
9oz (275g) white cabbage, coarsely
*   shredded*
8 chive sprigs

Seafood

A great mid-week meal. Serve this with a fresh garden salad—no fuss and so quick to make.

THUNFISCH FRIKADELLEN

SERVES 4

Tuna Fishcakes

1lb (500g) potatoes
1½ tablespoons (20g) butter
2 tablespoons parsley, chopped
2 scallions, chopped
cilantro, chopped
½lb (200g) tuna chunks
2 tablespoons all-purpose flour
salt and pepper
½lb (200g) breadcrumbs
oil, for frying

Boil the potatoes until soft, drain, and mash with the butter.

Mix the parsley, scallions, cilantro, potatoes, and tuna chunks together well.

Gradually add the flour and continue mixing until the mixture is well combined.

Season with salt and pepper.

Place the breadcrumbs in a bowl.

Form the tuna mixture into 8 patties and toss them in the breadcrumbs until well coated.

Fry the patties in a frying pan with oil until golden brown on both sides and the breadcrumbs have formed a crispy outer layer.

Pickled herring is a popular fish in Germany—particularly Hamburg, where I spent many years as a child. As a seaport, Hamburg enjoys much produce fresh from the sea.

ROLLMOPS MIT KARTOFFEL-TOMATEN-SALAT

SERVES 4

Pickled Herring *with Potato and Tomato Salad*

11oz (350g) fingerling potatoes
4 rollmop herrings
¼lb (110g) semi-dried tomatoes, chopped
⅓ cup (80ml) extra virgin-olive oil

Scrub the potatoes and place them in a saucepan of water. Bring to a boil and cook until tender. Leave to cool.

Unwrap the rollmops, keeping all the onion inside, and place them on a plate.

Quarter the potatoes and mix in with the tomatoes. Drizzle with olive oil.

Serve potato and tomato mixture alongside the herrings.

This salad is stylish enough for entertaining, yet so simple to prepare. The delicious combination of citrus fruits is sure to please the tastebuds.

LACHSFILET MIT FRÜHKARTOFFELN UND ZITRUSFRUCHTSALAT

Seared Fillet of Salmon with Potatoes and Citrus Salad

Boil the potatoes in salted water for approximately 12 to 15 minutes until just tender, then drain and allow them to cool a little before slicing. Season and drizzle over a little of the olive oil over the potatoes.

Drain the orange and lemon segments, reserving the juices, and remove to a separate bowl. Add seven tablespoons olive oil to the reserved juices and whisk together to combine, then season. Heat a non-stick frying pan and add the remaining olive oil. Season the salmon fillets and add to the pan, cooking them for about 3 to 4 minutes until seared and lightly golden. Flip over and cook for another minute until just tender.

Transfer to a plate and keep warm. Tip orange and lemon segments into the dressing and add the cilantro and arugula. Toss.

Place the salmon fillets onto serving plates, alongside the potatoes, and top with the arugula salad.

16 small fingerling potatoes, scrubbed clean
salt and pepper
½ cup (125ml) olive oil
3 oranges, peeled and segmented
3 lemons, peeled and segmented
4 salmon fillets, skinned
⅓ cup chopped cilantro
½lb (200g) arugula leaves

Cod is abundant in the North Sea and this firm white-skinned fish is just perfect to serve with mustard sauce. It is featured in many German recipes and is also my father's favorite dish.

KABELJAU IN SENFSOSSE

Cod *in Mustard Sauce*

Sprinkle the lemon juice over the cod fillets.

Combine the zest, onion, clove, and bay leaf in a pan. Slowly pour in the water and bring to a boil, then reduce heat, cover, and simmer for 20 minutes.

Add the cod fillets to the pan. Cover and cook on low for 10 minutes.

To make the mustard sauce, ladle one cup of the cooking liquid into a saucepan and gently simmer until the liquid has reduced by half. Stir in the mustard, add the butter, and whisk until all the ingredients are well combined. Add the parsley and season.

Place the cod fillets on a serving plate and pour on the mustard sauce. Garnish with a bay leaf or two and serve immediately with boiled potatoes and asparagus.

juice and zest of 1 lemon
4 good-sized cod fillets
1 white onion
1 clove
1 bay leaf
5 cups water
¼ cup good quality wholegrain mustard
8 tablespoons (125g) butter
½ cup chopped flat-leaf parsley
salt and pepper
bay leaves

Salmon is perfect for marinating and grilling. Try this easy dish served alongside mashed potatoes, potato gratin, garden salad with honey mustard dressing, or cooked beans.

MARINIERTE LACHSSTEAKS IN ROTWEINESSIG

SERVES 4

Marinated Salmon Steaks in Red Wine Vinegar

4 salmon fillets

butter

2 tablespoons breadcrumbs

salt and pepper

2 tablespoons parsley

MARINADE

½ white onion, chopped

½ Spanish onion, chopped

3 cloves garlic, crushed

3 bay leaves

2 tablespoon mixed dried herbs

scant ½ cup (100ml) red wine
  vinegar

scant ½ cup (100ml) olive oil

salt and pepper

Combine the marinade in a bowl. Place the salmon in the marinade, cover, and keep it in the marinade for approximately two hours.

Preheat the broiler. Remove the salmon from the marinade and place on a buttered baking tray. Brush with melted butter, sprinkle with the breadcrumbs, and season with salt and pepper.

Place under a the broiler for five minutes, until cooked. Garnish with parsley and serve.

Hamburg is a seaport and I remember visiting the fish markets there with my father as a young child. Fish is a traditional favorite in Hamburg. This goulash is somewhere between a stew and a soup— great for a cold winter's night, served with rustic bread and butter.

FISCHGULASCH

SERVES 6

Fish Goulash

4½lb (2kg) mixed fresh fish
2 white onions, chopped
4 cloves garlic, crushed
1 leek, chopped
3 teaspoons Hungarian paprika
salt, to taste
1 green pepper, seeded and sliced
  lengthways
1 red pepper, seeded and sliced
  lengthways
14oz (400g) can good quality diced
  tomatoes
2 stalks celery, chopped
½ cup white wine (preferably Riesling)
sour cream
parsley

Skin and fillet the fish, refrigerate the fillets, then place all the bones, fish heads, and skin into a large pan along with the onions, garlic, leek, paprika, and salt. Cover with water and bring to a boil, then reduce the heat and simmer for one to one and a half hours. Strain the stock thoroughly.

In a separate frying pan, combine the fish fillets, red and green peppers, tomatoes, and celery, and slowly add the fish stock. Cook gently on low heat, gradually adding the wine as it simmers. Cook for approximately 10 to 12 minutes.

Season to taste with salt and pepper, pour in to warm bowls, garnish with a dollop of sour cream and fresh chopped parsley, and serve immediately with sourdough or linseed bread.

Forelle Blau is a German specialty, often served on a bed of sauerkraut and caraway seeds and garnished with fresh bay leaves and lemon slices. This visually stunning dish is sure to delight guests at your next dinner party.

SERVES 4

FORELLE BLAU MIT PORREE

Oven-baked Trout *with* *White Wine Vinegar and Leeks*

Preheat the oven to 350°F (180°C).

Rub the skin of the trout with the sea salt and place in a roasting pan.

In a saucepan, bring the white wine vinegar to a boil and slowly pour this over the trout.

Rapidly cool the fish by fanning the pan or let it stand in a drafty place for five minutes.

Return to the heat until the vinegar is boiling and add the leeks, bay leaves, and peppercorns. Cover the roasting pan with aluminum foil and bake for about 30 minutes or until the fish is cooked.

Transfer the trout to individual plates and serve on a bed of sauerkraut with fresh bay leaves and lemon to garnish. Sprinkle with melted butter.

4 trout (around 6oz/185g each)
3 teaspoons sea salt
2½ cups white wine vinegar
2 leeks, sliced
2 bay leaves
8 whole black peppercorn
sauerkraut, to serve
bay leaves and lemon slices, to garnish
½ cup melted butter

You can never go wrong when serving smoked salmon. It goes wonderfully with potatoes, lemon, and dill. Serve warm with rye bread.

GERÄUCHERTER LACHS UND WARMER KARTOFFELSALAT MIT ZITRONEN-DILL-DRESSING

Smoked Salmon *and Warm Potato Salad*
with Lemon Dill Dressing

Boil, steam, or microwave the potatoes until cooked, then cover and keep warm.

Combine all the dressing ingredients in a large bowl then add in the potatoes. Gently mix in the salmon and season to taste.

Fill the iceberg lettuce cups with the potato salad and serve.

14oz (400g) baby potatoes, quartered
14oz (400g) smoked salmon slices
4 iceberg lettuce leaves

LEMON DILL DRESSING
2 tablespoons dill, finely chopped
1/3 cup (90ml) lemon juice
1 tablespoon olive oil
1 garlic clove, crushed
scant 1/2 cup (100ml) yogurt

This dish is light and fresh. Served with a fresh garden salad, it's great as an appetizer or light lunch. Enjoy with a glass of pinot grigio.

SAUTIERTE GARNELE MIT GRÜNER SOSSE

Sautéed Shrimp *with Green Sauce*

2¼lb (1kg) fresh uncooked shrimp
⅓ cup (80ml) olive oil
arugula, to serve

GREEN SAUCE
1 clove garlic, peeled
salt and pepper, to taste
1 bunch flat-leaf parsley, washed
    and dried
1 bunch basil, washed and dried
1 bunch chives, washed and dried
rosemary
½ teaspoon turmeric
mint, washed and dried
1 scallion
⅓ cup (80ml) olive oil
juice of ½ a lemon

To prepare the sauce, combine all the ingredients except the oil and juice in a blender. Pour in two to three tablespoons of the olive oil and the lemon juice, blend, and then add in an extra two to three tablespoons of water and the rest of the olive oil. Refrigerate in covered bowl for at least one hour before serving with the shrimp.

In a pan, sauté the fresh shrimp in the oil on high heat for three to four minutes until they have changed color but are still soft and fleshy to touch. Remove from the heat and let them cool slightly.

Arrange the shrimp on individual serving plates on a bed of fresh arugula with sauce on the side.

*This superb dish is really impressive looking and tastes great too!
It's great for dinner parties.*

SCHOLLE MIT HEISSER DILLSENFSOSSE

SERVES 4

Flounder *with Hot Dill Mustard Sauce*

olive oil

4 medium flounder, washed and
  dried

½ bunch dill, finely chopped

2 lemons, sliced into wedges

HOT DILL MUSTARD SAUCE

2½ tablespoons (35g) butter

4½ tablespoons (40g) flour

2 cups (500ml) fish stock

¼ cup (60ml) hot mustard

2 egg yolks

salt and white pepper

pinch of sugar

1 tablespoon white wine vinegar

1 tablespoon lemon juice

To prepare the sauce, fry the butter and flour in a pan until golden in color.

Add the fish stock, while stirring. Slowly simmer for 15 to 20 minutes, stirring occasionally. Mix the mustard, egg yolks, salt and pepper, sugar, white wine vinegar, and lemon juice together. Take the sauce off the heat and slowly add the mustard mixture to it, gently combining all the ingredients together.

Preheat a large frying pan and brush with the olive oil. Add the flounder to the pan and brush each side with a little of the olive oil. Pan fry for three to four minutes or until cooked through.

Arrange four plates and transfer a flounder to each plate. Pour the sauce over the flounder and garnish with fresh dill and lemon wedges.

Serve with herby sautéed baby potatoes and seasonal greens.

Meat, Game, & Poultry

The schnitzel is a traditional dish of the homeland and my personal favorite.

HÄHNCHENSCHNITZEL

Chicken Schnitzel

Wash the chicken breasts, pat dry with paper towel, and place on a clean chopping board.

Trim off unwanted fat and membrane then butterfly each chicken breast: position the breast so that its tip is facing you. Place your non-cutting hand on top of the breast. Insert your knife into the thickest part of the breast and slice into it until the knife reaches the middle. Make sure that the knife is cutting through two equal thicknesses of the breast. Open it like a book.

Place into a fridge to cool and rest the meat.

Use a mallet to flatten the chicken breast.

Prepare three flat, wide trays. Place flour in one, beaten egg in the second, and breadcrumbs in the third.

Dip the breasts into the flour, shake off any excess flour, dip into the egg, and then into the crumbs.

Fry in the oil until brown all over and cooked through.

4 chicken breasts
1 egg
½ cup all-purpose flour
2 cups good quality breadcrumbs
vegetable oil

Rustic, tasty, and tender, a delicious German favorite.

RINDERROULADEN

Beef Rouladen

1 lb (500g) round steak ½in (1cm) thick

salt and pepper

¼ cup (60ml) Dijon mustard

6 slices prosciutto

1 red onion, chopped

½ cup chopped dill pickle

2 cups flour

olive oil

¾ cup (200ml) beef stock

scant ½ cup (100ml) red wine

1 cup water

2 rosemary sprigs

flour or cornstarch

2 tablespoons sour cream or yogurt

curly parsley

Cut the steak into pieces, 2 x 4in (5 x 10cm), then pound until the steak is very thin.

Season strips with salt and pepper and spread a thin layer of Dijon mustard on one side.

Chop prosciutto into small pieces. Place one tablespoon of red onion, one tablespoon of prosciutto pieces, and one tablespoon of chopped dill pickle in the middle of each steak. Roll the steak up and thread a toothpick into the meat to hold the steak roll together. Repeat until all meat is rolled.

Place flour into a mixing bowl and coat individual rouladen on all sides.

In a large frying pan or baking pot, cook the rolls in olive oil. Add the beef stock, red wine, and water to a depth of half an inch. Add the rosemary sprigs. Cover the pan and simmer, adding more water and beef stock as needed to keep the meat covered. Turn rouladen from time to time in the sauce. Cook on low heat for about one hour or until tender. Remove to a heated serving dish.

Preheat oven to 325°F (160°C).

Thicken the gravy with a little flour or cornflour. Add sour cream or yogurt then pour over the rouladen and place in the oven for a further 5 to 10 minutes.

Garnish with curly parsley and serve with mashed potatoes, spätzel or noodles, and honey-glazed carrots.

VARIATIONS ON ROULADEN STUFFING

§ prosciutto, Swiss cheese, and spinach

§ smoked ham, gruyere cheese, and wholegrain mustard

§ red pepper, bacon, spinach, and cheddar cheese

A traditional German meat dish that originates from the south of Germany—an authentic dish.

DEUTSCHE ROULADEN

German Rouladen

Cut the flank steak into thin fillets, about 4in (10cm) thick and 3in (8cm) wide, then pound until they are very thin. Generously spread one side of each fillet with mustard.

Place bacon, onions, and pickle slices on each fillet and form into a roll. Use string or toothpicks to hold the roll together.

Heat a frying pan over medium heat and melt the butter. Place the rolls in the butter and sauté until browned.

Pour in two and a half cups of water and the bouillon cube, stirring to dissolve. Simmer for about one hour.

1½lb (750g) flank steak
1½ tablespoons Dijon or wholegrain mustard
½lb (250g) thick sliced bacon
2 large onions, sliced
dill or garlic pickle slices
2 tablespoons butter
2½ cups water
1 cube beef bouillon

Schmor is "braised" and brata is "roasted" in German. A great winter dish—beef and beer go together here like magic.

RINDFLEISCH SCHMORBRATEN GESCHMORT IN DUNKEL WEISS BEIR

SERVES 4–6

Beef Pot Roast *Braised in Dark Lager Beer*

3lb (1½kg) chuck roast

salt and pepper

olive oil

1 can dark beer

2 tablespoons paprika

1 teaspoon garlic, crushed

2 bay leaves

12 peppercorns

1 red bell pepper, chopped

1 green bell pepper, chopped

3lb (1½kg) baby potatoes

2 large onions, quartered

Season the roast and brown in a large frying pan with olive oil.

Pour a little dark beer into the bottom of a slow cooker, before placing the roast inside. Pour in the remainder of the dark beer then add the paprika, garlic, bay leaves, peppercorns, and peppers and turn the slow cooker to high. Add the whole baby potatoes and onions and cook for three to six hours until the meat separates easily with a fork. Serve with fresh sauerkraut or red cabbage on the side.

This is an exellent dish that has a great texture.

HUHN MIT WALNUSS-SALAT

Chicken and Walnut Salad

1 lb (500g) cooked chicken, chopped
2 celery sticks, coarsely chopped
1 large apple, cored and diced
½ cup of walnuts, roughly chopped
⅓ cup mayonnaise
1–2 tablespoons cream, optional
watercress sprigs

Place the chicken in a large bowl with the celery, apple, and walnuts. Thin the mayonnaise if necessary by adding a small amount of cream to give the consistency of heavy cream.

Pour over the chicken and toss well until the ingredients are evenly coated. Turn into a serving dish and garnish with watercress.

Serve this with garlic mashed potatoes and green beans. This is seriously tasty.

SERVES 4

HÄHNCHENBRUST IN SAHNIGER PILZOSSE

Chicken Breast *and Creamy Mushroom Sauce*

Divide each chicken breast into two fillets, place them between two sheets of plastic wrap, and flatten with a rolling pin to a thickness of ½in (1cm). Cut into 1in (2½cm) strips diagonally across the fillets.

Heat 2 tablespoons of the oil in a frying pan and cook the onion slowly until soft but not browned. Add the mushrooms and cook until golden brown. Remove from the pan and keep warm.

Increase the heat, add the remaining oil and fry the chicken quickly, in small batches, for about 3 to 4 minutes until lightly colored. Return the onions and mushrooms to the pan and season with the salt and black pepper. Stir in the sour cream and bring to a boil. Sprinkle with fresh tarragon and serve.

4 large chicken breasts
3 tablespoons (45ml) olive oil
1 large onion, thinly sliced
3 cups mushrooms, sliced
salt and black pepper
1¼ cups sour cream
1 tablespoon fresh tarragon, chopped

The mustard in this dish gives the sauce an edge. The sauce simply transforms the chicken breast into a delectable meal.

SERVES 4

HÄHNCHENBRUST IN SENF-SALBEI-SOSSE

Chicken Breast *with Creamy Mustard and Sage Sauce*

Cut the chicken into strips, then heat the oil and butter in the pan and sauté the chicken over medium heat until lightly golden.

In a saucepan, heat the stock and the cream. Stir in the Dijon and wholegrain mustard and the sage. Squeeze in the juice, if using.

Serve with fresh green beans and mashed potatoes.

1lb (500g) chicken breast

1 teaspoon oil

1 teaspoon butter

1 cup (250ml) chicken stock

1 cup (250ml) cream

1 tablespoon Dijon mustard

3 tablespoons wholegrain mustard

1 tablespoon freshly chopped sage

juice of ½ lemon or lime, optional

*Great with mashed potato or pasta this is a good family meal—
quick and easy to make, it will warm you from the inside out.*

HÄHNCHEN STROGANOFF

Chicken Stroganoff

4 large chicken breasts

¼ cup (60ml) olive oil

1 large onion, thinly sliced

3 cups mushrooms, sliced

salt and black pepper

1¼ cups sour cream

1 tablespoon fresh parsley, chopped

Divide each chicken breast into two fillets, place them between two sheets of plastic wrap and flatten with a rolling pin to a thickness of ½in (1cm). Cut into 1in (2½cm) strips diagonally across the fillets.

Heat 2 tablespoons of the oil in a frying pan and cook the onion slowly until soft but not browned. Add the mushrooms and cook until golden brown. Remove from the pan and keep warm.

Increase the heat, add the remaining oil, and fry the chicken quickly, in small batches, for about 3 to 4 minutes until lightly browned. Return the onions and mushrooms to the pan and season with the salt and black pepper. Stir in the sour cream and bring to a boil. Sprinkle with fresh parsley and serve.

SELBST GEMACHTE HÜHNERBRÜHE

Homemade Chicken Stock

Fill a large pot with the water and add the chicken pieces. Bring to a boil then reduce the heat to simmer, skimming any fat from the surface.

Add the onion, celery, leek, bay leaves, and seasoning and simmer over low heat for 2 hours.

Strain the stock into a large bowl and allow to cool then refrigerate or freeze in portions

1 free-range chicken, cut into pieces
13 cups (3 liters) water
1 onion
2 celery sticks
1 leek
2 bay leaves
freshly ground pepper, to taste

This dish is sure to please and easy to make. Honey and mustard are ingredients found in most household pantries. Serve with boiled pototoes and diced carrots for an authentic meal.

SERVES 4

HONIG-SENF-HÄHNCHEN

Honey Mustard Chicken

Place the chicken in a bowl with the olive oil, lemon juice, salt and pepper, mustard, and honey. Marinate in the fridge for one hour.

Fry the onion and zest in a large pan until the onion is soft. Add the chicken and cook on both sides until golden. Pour in the stock and wine, add the bay leaf, slowly bring to a boil, then simmer slowly for 20 minutes. Season to taste.

Garnish with flat-leaf parsley and serve with boiled baby potatoes and diced carrots.

8 chicken thighs
olive oil
juice and zest of 1 lemon
salt and pepper, to taste
2 teaspoons wholegrain mustard
1 tablespoon honey
1 onion
4¼ cups (1 liter) chicken stock
1 cup (250ml) white wine
1 bay leaf
¼ cup flat-leaf parsley

A zesty dish with fantastic aromas. Low in fat and simple to prepare.

ORANGEN-HONIG-HÄHNCHENBRUST

SERVES 4

Orange, Thyme, and Honey Chicken

4 chicken breasts
1 teaspoon olive oil
juice and zest of 3 oranges
3 teaspoons honey
1 teaspoon fresh thyme
salt and pepper

Sauté the chicken in a pan with the oil until golden on both sides.

In a bowl, combine the juice, zest, honey, and thyme.

Pour mixture into the pan over the chicken and simmer for a further ten minutes or until the chicken is cooked through. If desired, season with salt and pepper to taste.

Serve with baked baby potatoes and a fresh apple and pear salad.

Serve with a crisp green salad and baby potatoes. Or try this with spätzle, a traditional German noodle. Delicious authentic cuisine.

SPECK-SAUERKRAUT-TOMATEN-HÄHNCHEN

SERVES 4

Simmered Bacon, Sauerkraut, and Tomato Chicken

1 teaspoon olive oil

1 large white onion, diced

4 rashers bacon, diced

2 cloves garlic

4 chicken breasts

2 x 14oz (400g) cans diced tomato

1 tablespoon tomato paste

½lb (250g) sauerkraut

½ cup white wine (preferably Riesling)

salt and pepper

fresh curly parsley

Sauté the diced onion and bacon in the oil over high heat until the bacon starts to color. Add the garlic and continue to cook for a further two minutes or until the onion is soft.

Add the chicken and cook for two minutes each side until golden brown. Add the canned tomato, tomato paste, and sauerkraut. Pour in the white wine, stir, and cook for a further 8 minutes.

Season to taste then simmer over low heat for a further ten minutes.

Garnish with fresh parsley and serve with spätzle or noodle.

This dish is particularly good served with hot potatoes baked in their skins and sour cream or with French bread.

EINGELEGTES SCHWEINEFLEISCH

Mulled Pork

Place all the ingredients in a large pan or ideally in a slow cooker and place it in the fridge overnight. If cooking the same evening leave as long as possible. (Slow cookers can be set on low before going to work or high if cooking that evening.)

If using a good old-fashioned pot, set it on the heat, bring to a boil, and simmer gently for 40 to 60 minutes.

When the meat is tender, check seasonings and consistency; if it is too liquid, remove the lid and reduce by turning up the heat or mix in a little arrowroot dissolved in water and stir in.

2¼lb (1kg) pork shoulder or
  foreloin, diced
3 cups (750ml) red wine
2½ tablespoons brandy
juice and zest of 2 oranges
juice and zest of 1 lemon
1 tablespoon soft brown sugar
6 cloves
6 juniper berries
½ cup golden raisins
1 tablespoon beef stock powder
4 apples, sliced
3 onions, sliced
4 cloves garlic, crushed
2 teaspoons cinnamon
2 teaspoons nutmeg
salt and pepper, to taste

Deliciously indulgent and mouthwatering.

SCHWEINEKOTELETT IN SENFSOSSE

Pork Chops *with Mustard Sauce*

Melt the butter in a frying pan, add the onion, and sauté until soft. Remove from the pan and set aside.

Season the flour with salt and pepper and coat the chops with the mixture. Add the floured chops to the pan and fry both sides until golden brown.

Return the onion to the pan and pour in the sherry and chicken stock. Cover and simmer on low heat for 30 minutes or until the chops are cooked.

Stir in the mustard, season to taste, and garnish with fresh rosemary.

2 tablespoons (30g) butter
1 onion, finely chopped
4 pork chops
1 tablespoon flour
salt and pepper
½ cup medium sherry
¾ cup (190ml) chicken stock
2 tablespoons light Dijon mustard
fresh rosemary

A fantastic and appealing dish. The freshly stewed plums marry beautifully with the pork. Serve with seasonal vegetables.

SCHWEINSFILET MIT GEDÄMPFTEN PFLAUMEN

Pork Fillet *with Freshly Stewed Plums*

Preheat the oven to 350°F (180°C).

Season the flour with salt and pepper and use to coat the pork.

Melt the butter in a frying pan, add the pork, and fry until golden brown on both sides. Transfer to a casserole dish.

Mash the plums to a coarse purée, stir in the cinnamon and wine, then pour over the pork.

Cover and cook in the oven for 30 minutes then serve hot, garnished with the parsley.

2 tablespoons all-purpose flour

salt and pepper

1 lb (500g) pork fillet, cut into 4 pieces

4 tablespoons (60g) butter

1 x 14oz (425g) can purple plums, drained and pitted

¼ teaspoon ground cinnamon

⅔ cup (160ml) red wine

parsley, chopped

Another simple and delicious meal—homestyle cooking at its best. Sage and cider pair perfectly with the pork. Serve this dish straight from the casserole dish at the table.

Salbei-Schweinefleisch in Apfelwein

SERVES 10

Sage Pork *in Cider*

scant ½ cup (100g) butter

2 large onions, sliced

4 apples, sliced

¼ cup arrowroot

2 teaspoons beef stock powder

2¼lb (1kg) pork shoulder or foreloin, diced

3 cups (750ml) dry hard cider

2 teaspoons sugar

¼ cup apple concentrate

1½ tablespoons fresh sage, chopped, or 1 tablespoon dried (or to taste)

salt and pepper, to taste

dash of calvados

Melt half the butter in a large frying pan and fry the onion until soft. Add the apples and continue cooking gently for a further five to ten minutes. Transfer to a casserole or slow cooker.

Combine the arrowroot and the stock powder and use it to coat the pork. Heat the remaining butter and brown the pork, sealing the edges.

Add the diced pork, hard cider, sugar, apple concentrate, and sage to the pot and simmer for approximately 40 minutes. Once the meat is tender, add the salt and pepper, more sage if desired, and a dash of calvados.

This dish is a favorite of my father's. Serve over a bed of mashed potatoes with plenty of sauce.

Omas Paprika-Schweinekotelett

Grandma's Paprika Pork Cutlets

4 x 6oz (180g) pork cutlets

salt

¼ cup (60ml) oil

3½oz (100g) bacon or speck, diced

1 white onion

2 tablespoons tomato paste

4 green peppers, thinly sliced

1 tablespoon mild paprika

¾ cup (200g) sour cream

fresh parsley

Place pork cutlets on a chopping board and lightly salt.

Add the oil to a frying pan and cook the cutlets on medium heat until cooked through. Remove from the pan and set aside.

Add diced bacon or speck and the onion to the pan. Sauté until the bacon is slightly golden and the onion is soft. Add the tomato paste, peppers, and paprika, stir and lower the heat to a simmer, then stir in the sour cream and mix well.

Place the cutlets back in the pan and cook on low heat for a further 10 minutes.

Arrange the cutlets on a plate over a bed of mashed potatoes. Pour on the sauce and garnish with fresh parsley.

Serve immediately with a side of red cabbage or seasonal greens.

A great combination of traditional German fare and a sustaining and warming dish that wakes the tastebuds.

SCHWEINEFLEISCH MIT SAUERKRAUT

Pork Stew *with Sauerkraut*

Heat the oil in a large pan and brown the onion and crushed garlic cloves until soft.

Add the pork cubes to the pan and fry until browned. Stir in the caraway seeds and fresh dill and pour in the stock. Cook for 1 hour over low heat.

Stir the drained sauerkraut into the pork with the paprika. Let it simmer for 45 minutes. Add salt to taste.

Garnish the stew with a little more dill and serve with sour cream, sprinkled with paprika.

2 tablespoons vegetable oil

2 onions, finely chopped

2 garlic cloves, crushed

2¼lb (1 kg) lean pork, cut into
   2in (5cm) cubes

1 teaspoon caraway seeds

2 tablespoons fresh dill, chopped

3¾ cups warm pork or vegetable
   stock

4 cups sauerkraut, drained

1 tablespoon paprika, plus extra to
   serve

salt

sour cream

KALBSROULADEN

Veal Rolls

Preheat the oven to 350°F (180°C).

Place the veal or pork between two pieces of plastic wrap and pound with a rolling pin or mallet to flatten to a regular shape. Season well.

Top each slice with a layer of bacon and ham. Beat the eggs in a small pan with the milk and stir over low heat until softly scrambled. Let cool.

Layer the scrambled eggs on top of each slice and spread with a knife, then sprinkle on the pickles. Roll up each slice carefully. Tie the rolls securely at intervals with string.

On the stovetop, melt butter in a large casserole dish. Add the meat rolls and brown all over. Remove the pan from the heat and put the rolls on to a plate. Spread the flour into the pan and stir thoroughly. Put the pan back on heat and cook flour mixture until light brown, then slowly add half of the water or stock. Return the meat rolls to the pan and bring to a boil, then place casserole in the oven for 1¾ to 2 hours to roast slowly, adding in the remaining water during cooking if necessary to stop the meat drying out.

When cooked, let the rolls cool for ten minutes before slicing. Serve with gravy and baby carrots, green beans, and dill pickles.

3lb (1¼kg) shoulder of veal or lean pork, cut into ½in (1½cm) slices

salt and freshly ground black pepper

½lb (230g) bacon

6oz (170g) sliced ham

4 beaten eggs

¼ cup (60ml) milk

3 dill pickles, finely diced

8 tablespoons (125g) butter

¼ cup self-rising flour

1½ cups (375ml) water or chicken stock

Creamy and delicious, this is a real favorite of mine. Serve with spätzle (a traditional German noodle) or plain white rice. This is a perfect, cozy dinner party option, as it can be prepared in advance.

SERVES 4

OMAS KALBFLEISCH STROGANOFF

Grandma's Veal Stroganoff

Pound the meat until soft then cut into thin strips.

Melt half the butter in a frying pan over low heat. Add the onion and the whole mushroom caps and stir in the tomato paste and flour. Stir over low heat for two to three minutes, then set aside.

In a clean frying pan, heat the remaining butter, add the veal, and fry over high heat, turning until evenly browned. Lower the heat, add the sauce to the pan followed by the sour cream, salt, pepper, lemon juice, and a splash of wine, then return to medium heat. Gently stir.

Garnish with fresh watercress and serve immediately with noodles or plain white rice.

4 veal cutlets

4 tablespoons (60g) butter

1 large white onion, diced

½lb (250g) button mushrooms, stalks removed

2 tablespoons tomato paste

1 tablespoon all-purpose flour

½ cup sour cream

salt and pepper

2 tablespoons lemon juice

splash of port or red wine, to taste

1 bunch watercress

Just delicious! Veal schnitzel is a breaded veal cutlet often served with fresh parsley and a lemon wedge. You can vary this dish by adding a mushroom sauce, or a spicy tomato-based pepper sauce.

Kalbsschnitzel

SERVES 4

Veal Schnitzel

4 veal cutlets, thinly sliced

salt and pepper

1 egg

½ cup all-purpose flour

2 cups good quality breadcrumbs

vegetable oil

Place the veal between two pieces of plastic wrap and pound with a rolling pin or mallet to flatten to ¼in (½cm). Season well and set aside. (The pounding helps to tenderize the meat.)

Prepare three flat, wide trays. Place flour in one, beaten egg in the second, and breadcrumbs in the third.

Dip the veal into the flour and shake off any excess, then dip into the egg, followed by the breadcrumbs, pressing gently into them to ensure the meat is well coated.

Heat the oil in a frying pan and place the veal into the pan; there should be enough oil for the meat to swim in it.

Fry over medium heat on both sides until the meat is cooked and the breadcrumb coating is crisp and golden brown. For the perfect schnitzel, the oil should be hot enough to brown it in 3 minutes. Serve immediately.

Meat Loaf is such a wonderful comfort food. I remember my mother making this on many a cold winter's day. It goes nicely with a good quality relish or chutney. It can also be sliced and eaten with freshly cut bread and salad.

FALSCHER HASE

Meat Loaf

1 tablespoon oil

3 bacon rashers, finely chopped

2 cloves garlic, diced

½ brown onion, diced

½ red onion, diced

5 slices bread

¾ cup milk

2¼lb (1kg) lean ground meat

2 free-range eggs

3 tablespoons (50g) tomato paste

salt and pepper

flat-leaf parsley, finely chopped

Preheat oven to 350°F (180°C).

Heat the oil in a frying pan, add the bacon, garlic, and the brown and red onion. Sauté until the onion is soft then set aside to cool.

Cut the bread into cubes, place in a bowl, and pour milk over it. Leave to soak until the milk is absorbed by the bread.

In a large bowl, combine the onion and bacon mixture, the bread mixture, the ground meat, eggs, tomato paste, and salt and pepper and mix well, then add the parsley.

Oil a loaf pan well and spoon the meatloaf mixture into it. Bake for 50 to 60 minutes or until cooked through. Let it stand to cool for five to ten minutes before slicing.

Garnish freely with fresh flat-leaf parsley and serve immediately with fresh seasonal vegetables or fresh garden salad with relish and chutney on the side.

This is a delightful dish—great for that special event to be celebrated in style. Surround the duck with baked potatoes, onions, and carrots.

SERVES 4–6

Duck *with Sauerkraut and Apple Stuffing*

Preheat the oven to 350°F (180°C).

In a frying pan, heat the oil and sauté the onion until transparent. Add the apples and cook until golden.

Stir in the brown sugar, salt and freshly ground pepper, half the thyme, and the caraway seeds, then add the sauerkraut to the pan and toss through the mixture over medium heat.

Leave to cool.

Prepare the duck by wiping the skin inside and out with a damp cloth or absorbent paper. Rub the duck with the remaining olive oil and season with salt and pepper.

Stuff the duck with the sauerkraut and apple mixture. Truss the duck, prick well with a fork, and place on a rack in a roasting pan. Roast for two to two and a half hours, remembering to prick the skin and baste every 30 minutes to allow the fat to escape.

Serve on a platter garnished with watercress and fresh apple slices.

2 tablespoons olive oil

1 large Spanish onion, coarsely chopped

2 cooking apples, peeled, cored, and diced

2 tablespoons brown sugar

salt and freshly ground pepper

bunch fresh thyme

1 teaspoon caraway seeds

1½lbs (700g) sauerkraut

4–5lb (1¾–2¼kg) duck

watercress

1 apple, sliced

Beautiful served with roasted baby potatoes and red cabbage.

SERVES 4–6

Lamb Steaks *with Fresh Apricot Sauce*

To make the sauce, pour the nectar into a shallow frying pan and bring to a boil. Add the dried apricots, honey, mint, and lemon zest and juice. Simmer on low for 20 minutes, stirring occasionally.

Preheat the broiler. Mix the honey with the oil and lightly brush over the steaks. Season with salt and pepper. Broil for four to five minutes each side for medium-rare. If you prefer well-done, broil for a few more minutes.

Garnish each steak with a sprig of mint and serve on a pool of sauce.

2 tablespoons honey
2 tablespoons olive oil
4–6 5oz (150g) lamb steaks
salt and ground black pepper
fresh mint, to garnish

APRICOT SAUCE
13fl oz (400ml) can apricot nectar
½ cup dried apricots
2 tablespoons honey
2 tablespoons chopped mint
½ teaspoon grated lemon zest
1 tablespoon lemon juice

Nürnberger is an authentic German sausage from Nuremberg. It is a relatively small pork sausage (about 3¼in/8cm). You'll find street vendors in Nuremberg that sell this in a bread roll, often with sauerkraut. You can find these sausages in any good German butcher or delicatessen.

SERVES 4

GESCHMORTE NÜRNBERGER WÜRSTCHEN MIT LINSEN

Nuremberg Sausage *and Lentil Braise*

Preheat the oven to 350°F (180°C).

In a frying pan, sauté the carrots and parsnips in a tablespoon of the olive oil, then place in a baking tray and season with salt, pepper, and half the thyme and rosemary. Roast the vegetables in the oven for approximately 25 minutes, turning once until golden and cooked through.

While the vegetables are roasting, sauté the sausages in the frying pan in more of the oil until golden; then set aside.

Drain the oil from the pan, leaving only one tablespoon to sauté the remaining ingredients. Sauté the onion over low heat for approximately 20 minutes until soft and tender. Add in the garlic, brown sugar, balsamic vinegar, and the remaining two tablespoons of thyme and rosemary and sauté for a minute or two. Stir in the beef stock, red wine, and lentils and cook for a further five to ten minutes. Serve, garnished with parsley.

1 bunch young carrots, peeled

2 parsnips, peeled and cut lengthways

2-3 tablespoons (30-45ml) olive oil

salt and pepper

¼ cup chopped thyme leaves

¼ cup rosemary

10 Nürnberger sausages

2 onions, sliced in wedges

2 garlic cloves, crushed

1 teaspoon brown sugar

2 tablespoons balsamic vinegar

1 cup (250ml) beef stock

2½ tablespoons red wine

1 can brown lentils, rinsed and drained

3 teaspoons fresh flat-leaf parsley leaves

This can easily be frozen but only add the sour cream after it has been defrosted and warmed up. Great with noodles or rice or even as a baked potato filling.

HACKFLEISCHAUFLAUF

German Minced Meat Casserole

2 onions, diced

1 tablespoon oil

1 tablespoon butter

1 lb (500g) ground beef

1 leek, sliced

5 tablespoons tomato paste

1 cup (250ml) stock

1 tablespoon mustard

1 teaspoon mild paprika

1 teaspoon salt

¼ cup sour cream

In a casserole dish, fry the diced onion in the oil and butter over low heat. Turn up the heat and add the ground beef, stirring it until it is brown.

Add the leek, tomato paste, stock, mustard, and paprika and season to taste.

Simmer for about 15 minutes. Add the sour cream shortly before serving.

This simple, tasty dish makes a great mid-week meal.

Eierpfannkuchen mit Speck

Egg Cakes *with Bacon*

¼lb (125g) sliced bacon

4 eggs

1 tablespoon flour

⅓ cup (80ml) milk

 salt and ground pepper

1 bunch chives, chopped

Fry the bacon then remove from the pan and keep warm. Pour half of the bacon fat out of the pan.

Beat the eggs with the flour, milk, salt, and pepper.

Heat the remaining bacon fat in the pan. Pour in the egg mixture and leave it to cook. Lay the bacon slices on top of it. Briefly place the pan under the grill to brown the top.

To serve, sprinkle with chives and serve with salad and bread or bread rolls.

This recipe is from my grandmother and was a favorite of my father when he was a child. Great served with potatoes.

SERVES 4

Eggs *in Mustard Sauce*

In a pan, melt the butter over medium heat and add the flour. Stir continuously until golden in color. Be careful not to let the flour burn, as this will make the sauce bitter.

Gradually add the stock, a little at a time, stirring continuously. Mix in the sour cream and mustard, stirring until smooth. Bring the sauce to a boil, lower the heat, and simmer for 10 minutes. Add the salt, pepper, sugar, and nutmeg to taste, then stir in the chives.

Boil the eggs for 6 to 8 minutes, then immediately plunge them into cold water. Peel the eggs and put them into the sauce.

3 tablespoons (40g) butter or
  margarine
½ cup flour
1 cup (250ml) warm vegetable stock
1 cup (250g) sour cream
3 tablespoons mustard
salt and pepper
nutmeg
pinch of sugar
1 bunch chives, chopped
8 eggs

These go particularly well with potatoes and parsley or rice.

GEFÜLLTE PAPRIKASCHOTEN

Stuffed Peppers

Preheat oven to 400°F (200°C).

Cut a third off each pepper, lengthwise, and remove the seeds and internal membrane so you have a pepper shell. Finely slice the remaining pieces of pepper.

Mix together the ground beef, egg, chives, paprika, tomato paste, sliced pepper, half of the marjoram, and one tablespoon of the sour cream. Season with salt and pepper to taste.

Fill the peppers with the mixture, adding the remaining marjoram.

Place the peppers in a casserole dish, drizzle the oil over them, and add the stock to the dish. Bake for 50 minutes.

Remove the dish from oven, spoon out the sauce, and mix it in with the cornstarch over low heat. Add the rest of the sour cream and season with salt and pepper.

Serve the peppers with the sauce.

4 medium-sized bell peppers
11oz (300g) ground beef
1 egg
1 bunch chives, chopped
¼ teaspoon mild paprika
1 tablespoon tomato paste
6 stalks of marjoram
⅔ cup (150g) sour cream
salt and pepper
1 tablespoon oil
1 cup (250ml) stock
1 teaspoon cornstarch

Vegetables

A beautiful and tasty dish. These vegetables make a great accompaniment to many German dishes.

MÖHREN-PASTINAK-KOHL-GENÜSE MIT SENFKÖRNERN

Carrot, Parsnip, and Cabbage
with Mustard Seeds

Heat the oil in a frying pan and add the mustard seeds. They will start to pop instantly. Add the chili and stir for approximately one minute.

Add the carrots, parsnips, and cabbage. Toss over medium heat for two to three minutes, then add parsley and mint and toss again.

Season with salt, freshly ground pepper, and the sugar. Add the lemon juice, then taste and correct seasoning. Serve immediately.

¼ cup (60ml) sunflower oil

1 tablespoon black mustard seeds

1 chili pepper, seeded and chopped

½lb (225g) carrots, coarsely grated

½lb (225g) parsnips, grated

½lb (225g) cabbage, finely shredded
  against the grain

2 tablespoons parsley, chopped

2 tablespoons mint, freshly chopped

salt and freshly ground pepper

1 teaspoon sugar

2 tablespoons freshly-squeezed lemon
  juice, to taste

Slow-cooked and rich in vibrant color, this beautiful dish is sure to please! It makes an excellent accompaniment to roast pork or game. Vary the dish by using pears or a mix of apples and pears.

GESCHMORTER APFEL-ROTKOHL

SERVES 8

Braised Apple Red Cabbage

Preheat the oven to 325°F (160°C).

Cut the cabbage into quarters and cut out and discard the stalk. Finely shred the cabbage and place in a large saucepan of boiling water, ensuring there is enough water to cover it. Bring the water back to a boil and drain the cabbage. The cabbage will now appear an inky blue color. Don't be concerned; it will regain its color later, when the vinegar is added.

In a frying pan, sauté the onion in butter. Cook gently until transparent, then add the apple. Cook gently, stirring, for a further two to three minutes. Remove from the pan and set aside.

In an ovenproof casserole dish, combine the red cabbage and apple and onion mixture. Gently mix and layer together.

Mix together the vinegar, water, and sugar together and sprinkle over the dish. Note the

1 red cabbage

1 onion

butter

2 cooking apples, peeled, sliced, and diced

2 teaspoons white or red wine vinegar

2 tablespoons water

1 tablespoon sugar

salt and pepper

red color returning to the cabbage as the vinegar is added. Season with salt and pepper.

Cover the cabbage with buttered parchment paper and a lid and bake for one and a half hours or until tender, stirring occasionally and moistening with a little extra water, if necessary.

The cabbage should be lightly sweet and sour. It may be necessary to add more sugar or vinegar to suit your taste and achieve a wonderful result.

Refreshing and light. It's a great accompaniment to almost any German meal. A very popular dish of the homeland.

GURKENSALAT

SERVES 4–6

Cucumber Salad

2 medium cucumbers
1¼ cup chopped red onion
1 tablespoon herbs, freshly chopped

DRESSING
½ cup (125ml) apple cider vinegar
 or wine vinegar
2 tablespoons oil
2–3 tablespoons sugar
salt and pepper, to taste

Peel and slice the cucumber in ⅛in (¼cm) thick slices. Place on paper towel for 20 minutes to allow the water to wick out of the cucumber, then place in bowl.

To make the dressing, simmer the vinegar in a saucepan. Stir in the oil and sugar and season. Allow to cool.

Add red onion to cucumber, then mix in the dressing. Garnish with fresh herbs to serve.

KARTOFFELAUFLAUF MIT SPECK

Bacon and Potato Gratin

1 teaspoon sunflower oil

11oz (300g) bacon, diced

2 onions, diced

2 cloves garlic

*2 tablespoons chopped flat-leaf
    parsley*

3lb (1½kg) potatoes

butter

2 teaspoons wholegrain mustard

1 cup (250ml) heavy cream

salt and pepper

1 cup grated cheddar cheese

parsley, to garnish

Preheat oven to 400°F (200°C).

In a frying pan, heat the oil over medium heat. Add the bacon to the pan and sauté until golden, about five minutes. Remove the bacon from the pan and set aside.

Add the onion and garlic to pan and sauté until browned, about ten minutes. Combine with the bacon and stir in the parsley.

Grease an ovenproof dish with butter. Cut the potatoes in to ¼in (½cm) slices. Layer the potato slices with the bacon-onion mixture in the dish.

Stir the wholegrain mustard into the cream and pour over the potatoes. Season with sea salt and ground pepper.

Sprinkle the cheese over the top and cover with foil. Bake in the oven until cooked and the cheese is a golden color. Garnish with more parsley and serve immediately.

Just delicious. A rustic, wholesome summer salad.

Bohnen-Walnuss-Salat mit Speck

Green Bean, Bacon, and Walnut Salad

1½lb (750g) green beans, trimmed

3oz (80g) walnuts

3½oz (100g) bacon, diced

3 cloves garlic, chopped

1oz (30g) sesame seeds

2 teaspoons olive oil

3 tablespoons (40ml) apple cider vinegar

¾ cup flat-leaf parsley

salt and pepper

Fill a large pot with salted water and bring to a boil. Add the beans, reduce the heat to medium, and simmer until just tender, about 3 to 4 minutes. Drain, refresh under cold water, and set aside.

Preheat the oven to 350°F (180°C).

Place the walnuts on a small baking tray and roast until golden brown, approximately 7 minutes, then allow to cool.

Sauté the bacon and garlic over medium heat until cooked.

In a small mixing bowl, combine the walnuts, bacon, garlic, sesame seeds, olive oil, and vinegar.

Arrange the green beans on a serving dish and gently spoon the mixture over them. Add the parsley. Season to taste and serve immediately.

Bacon or onion may be diced and added to this dish for an extra kick.

KRAÜTER-KARTOFFELN

Mixed Herb Potatoes

Boil the potatoes in their skins then allow to cool. Once cool, cut into even quarters.

In a frying pan, heat the olive oil and add the potatoes. Season with salt and pepper to taste and sprinkle in the mixed herbs. Cook until golden brown, turning the potatoes regularly to ensure all sides are browned.

Serve garnished with fresh herbs.

3lb (1½kg) potatoes
½ cup (125ml) olive oil
sea salt and pepper
1 teaspoon mixed dried herbs
fresh parsley or rosemary

This goes well with mashed or boiled potatoes and cooked greens on the side. You'll need to begin this recipe a day ahead.

BRAUNE BOHNEN MIT KNUSPRIGEM SCHINKEN

Slow-baked Brown Beans
with Roasted Bacon

2½ cups dried Swedish brown beans

2¾lb (1¼kg) bacon joint

1 large brown onion, finely chopped

2 apples, peeled, cored, and finely
  diced

scant ½ cup (100ml) balsamic
  vinegar

⅓ cup soft brown sugar

1 cinnamon stick, broken in half

2 garlic cloves, finely chopped

1½ teaspoons Hungarian sweet
  paprika

1 teaspoon dried marjoram

1½ teaspoons caraway seeds, lightly
  crushed

Soak the beans in a generous amount of water overnight.

Bring a large saucepan of water to a boil and add the piece of bacon. Cook steadily for one hour, then remove the bacon to a plate and reserve the liquid.

Preheat the oven to 350°F (180°C). Drain the beans, then spread them in a large roasting pan with the onion. Pour in enough of the reserved cooking liquid to cover the beans, approximately three cups. Cover tightly with foil and cook in the oven for two and a half hours. Remove from the oven.

Stir in the apple, vinegar, sugar, cinnamon stick, and garlic. Place a roasting rack over the top, making sure the rack does not touch the beans.

Remove the rind from the bacon so that the fat layer is exposed. Combine the paprika, marjoram, and caraway and sprinkle over the top. Place bacon on the rack with the fat side facing up, and return to the oven.

Cook for 45 minutes, or until the bacon is very tender. If the beans are not saucy and thick by this stage, remove the bacon and keep warm.

Increase oven temperature to 400°F (200°C), and continue cooking for five to 10 minutes. Thickly slice the bacon and serve over the beans.

Photo on following page.

Pikantes Joghurt Relish

Spiced Yogurt Relish

1 red onion, thinly sliced

½ cucumber, seeded and thinly sliced

1 tablespoon cumin seeds, toasted

1 bunch cilantro (including stems),
   roughly chopped

2 tomatoes, quartered, seeded, and
   thinly sliced

1¾ cups (400ml) plain full-fat
   yogurt

salt and freshly ground black pepper

Combine onion and cucumber in a sieve, sprinkle generously with salt, and set in bowl for ten minutes. Rinse thoroughly and pat dry.

Combine the cucumber and onion with the cumin seeds, cilantro, tomatoes, and yogurt. Stir well and adjust the seasoning (usually there is enough salt from the cucumber and onion).

Cabbage has been known as poor man's fare, but it is such a glorious vegetable. It's low in cholestrol and rich in minerals, especially iron. This salad can be consumed hot or cold.

White Cabbage and Bacon Salad

1 white cabbage
scant ½ cup (100ml) olive oil
½ cup (125ml) white wine vinegar
1½ cups (375ml) warm water
1 teaspoon caraway seeds
3 tablespoons (50ml) white wine
3 rashes bacon or speck, diced
salt and pepper

Quarter the cabbage and remove the stalk, then wash thoroughly in salted water and drain well.

Cut the cabbage into fine strips and place in a large bowl. Add the olive oil, mix thoroughly to coat the cabbage, and let stand for one hour.

Mix the vinegar, warm water, caraway seeds, and wine together well and pour this over the cabbage. Cover for one to two hours.

Sauté the bacon in a pan until golden and add this to the cabbage salad, mix thoroughly, and season to taste.

This goes well with almost any dish. Vary the vegetables used and add fresh garden herbs to garnish and create that rustic, home-cooked fare that will tempt and delight the eye.

WINTERLICHES GEMÜSE IN WEISSWEINSOSSE

Winter Vegetables in White Wine

Heat the oil in a large frying pan over medium heat. Add bacon and cook until golden brown. Lower the heat and add the scallions and a pinch of salt. Cook for a further two minutes.

Add the carrots, celery, and zucchini then pour the wine and chicken stock over the vegetables. Cook and reduce over medium heat. Add tomato and cook for a further 5 to 10 minutes.

In two separate saucepans, gently boil the green beans and peas until semi-cooked. Drain and refresh in ice water

Add green beans and peas to the other vegetables and simmer for a further three to five minutes.

Garnish with fresh garden herbs and serve with mashed potatoes or gratin and your favorite meat.

2 tablespoons olive oil

3½oz (100g) bacon hock or smoked ham

3 scallions, sliced into batons

salt

1 large carrot, peeled and sliced into batons

1 celery stick, sliced

1 zucchini, sliced

1 cup fresh peas

½lb (250g) fresh green beans

2 fresh tomatoes, diced

scant ½ cup (100ml) Riesling or other white wine

scant ½ cup (100ml) homemade chicken stock

fresh herbs

Rösti can be served with smoked salmon and a dill and caper dressing or with fresh apple sauce as a sweet treat.

KARTOFFEPUFFER

Potato Rösti

Peel and finely grate the potatoes. Place them in a fresh clean dish towel and squeeze out any moisture.

In a bowl, combine the cream, egg yolk, and grated potato and season with salt, pepper, and nutmeg. Form into 12 potato cakes.

In a shallow pan, heat the oil over medium heat and fry the cakes, flattening each with a spatula and cooking on both sides until they are golden.

1¾lb (800g) potatoes
3½oz (100g) heavy cream
1 egg yolk
salt and freshly ground pepper
nutmeg
4 tablespoons oil

Dressings & Sauces

Great with seafood dishes, accompanied by fresh garden salad.

SCHNITTLAUCH-ZITRONEN-SENF-DRESSING

Fresh Chive, Lemon, and *Dijon Mustard Dressing*

⅓ cup (80ml) lemon juice

⅔ cup (150ml) extra virgin olive oil

1½ tablespoons Dijon mustard

2 tablespoons fresh chives, chopped

1 garlic clove, finely chopped

salt and pepper, to taste

Blend all the ingredients in a blender until combined.

Great with goat cheese salad, beans, and roasted beets.

KAPERN-DRESSING

MAKES APPROX. 1 CUP (240ML)

Caper Dressing

1 ½ tablespoons red wine vinegar
¾ cup (200ml) olive oil
3 garlic cloves, crushed
1 ½ tablespoons capers
sea salt and pepper

Whisk all ingredients in a small bowl until blended. Use immediately.

This dressing is delicious poured over hot and cold vegetables and salad. It is particularly yummy as a warm potato dressing.

CATHERINES SPEZIAL DRESSING

Catherine's Special Salad Dressing

Whisk all ingredients in a small bowl until blended. Use immediately.

2 free-range eggs
3 tablespoons wholegrain mustard
½ cup (125ml) red wine vinegar
¼ teaspoon paprika
1 teaspoon white sugar
1 cup (250ml) grapeseed oil
sea salt, to taste
1 teaspoon mayonnaise

MAKES APPROX. 1 CUP (250 ML)

MEERETTICHSOSSE

Horseradish Dressing

Whisk all ingredients in a small bowl until blended. Use immediately.

¾ cup horseradish sauce

3 teaspoons Dijon mustard

3 teaspoons chopped horseradish

1 tablespoon lemon juice

2 tablespoons water

AIOLI

Aioli

1 egg yolk
1 clove garlic, crushed
1 teaspoon Dijon mustard
1 teaspoon white wine vinegar
1 cup (250ml) olive oil
1 teaspoon lemon juice

Combine egg yolk, garlic, mustard, and white wine vinegar in a blender.

Gradually add the olive oil in a thin steady stream. Blend until the mixture thickens then add the lemon juice.

Desserts

A beautiful dessert on a hot day. This is a particularly popular dessert in Germany. Everyone just loves it—children especially.

FRUCHTPUDDING

Fruit Pudding

SERVES 6

½lb (250g) red currants
¼lb (125g) strawberries
¼lb (125g) red cherries
1 tablespoon sugar
2 tablespoons cornstarch

Wash the fruit and remove stems. Add fruits to a saucepan, along with a little bit of water and the sugar. Cook gently for ten minutes.

Mix the cornstarch with a little bit of cold water then add in to the fruit mixture. Allow it to cook for two minutes more to thicken.

Allow to cool slightly. Fill dessert dishes or glasses and place in the refrigerator to cool completely.

Serve with warm vanilla sauce or vanilla ice-cream.

Germany is a cake-loving country and this cake is very popular around Christmas time. It is perfect served with fresh coffee.

ROTWEINKUCHEN

Red Wine Cake

4 eggs

1¾ cups (250g) all-purpose flour

2 level teaspoons vanilla sugar

2½ level teaspoons baking powder

1 cup (200g) sugar

18 tablespoons (½lb/250g) butter

⅓ cup cinnamon

1–2 tablespoons cocoa

½ cup (125ml) red wine

3½oz (100g) grated chocolate

Preheat the oven to 350°F (180°C).

Mix together all the ingredients except the eggs and chocolate.

Separate the eggs, add the yolks into the mixture, and then beat the egg whites until stiff. Fold in the grated chocolate and then mix gently.

Place in a greased 8-inch (20-cm) round cake pan and bake for 50 to 60 minutes.

My mother used to bake this for afternoon tea, to share with her neighbors when they met for coffee on a Sunday.

SERVES 8–10

MUTTI'S KAFFEEKUCHEN

Mother's Coffee Cake

Preheat the oven to 350°F (180°C).

Mix the filling ingredients together and set aside.

To make the cake, beat the butter until fluffy, gradually add the sugar and vanilla sugar then add one egg at a time. Mix in the flour and baking powder then add the cream.

Put a third of the dough in an oiled and flour-dusted, 8-inch (20-cm) round cake pan. Spread half of the filling over it. Take another third of the cake mixture and place on top of the filling, then layer on the last of the filling, and then the last of the cake mix on top.

Use a fork to fold the mixture in one twist to form a slight pattern then bake for 60 minutes

After it has cooked, leave it to cool for 10 minutes before you take it out of the pan.

If you like, decorate with chocolate frosting or dust the top with confectioner's sugar.

FILLING
2/3 cup (150g) brown sugar
1 1/3 cup (125g) walnut meal
1 teaspoon cinnamon

*18 tablespoons (1/2lb/ 250g) butter
 or margarine*
1 1/2 cups (300g) sugar
2 teaspoons vanilla sugar
2 eggs
2 1/2 cups (350g) all-purpose flour
2 teaspoons baking powder
3/4 cup (200ml) heavy cream

My mother often made this for me as a child. It is an afternoon treat for the whole family to enjoy.

SERVES 10

KALTER HUND

Cold Dog

Chop the dark chocolate into small pieces and heat it up in a saucepan over low heat with the coconut oil, stirring constantly until melted; add the confectioner's sugar, almonds, and milk chocolate and mix.

Line a rectangular cake pan (8in/20cm long) with aluminum foil. Lay enough of the shortbead cookies in to cover the bottom, then pour over a layer of the chocolate mixture approximately ¾in (2cm) deep. Repeat the layers until all the mixture is used.

Leave it in the refrigerator for about three hours. Remove from the pan and slice to serve. Cut gently to ensure the cookies do not crumble.

3½oz (100g) dark chocolate
¼lb (125g) coconut oil
⅔ cup (75g) confectioner's sugar
1½oz (40g) almonds, chopped
2 tablespoons chopped milk chocolate
15 shortbread cookies

This cake is just delicious served with custard or whipped cream. It is lovely to bake for an afternoon with family and good friends.

Schokoladen-Kirsch-Kuchen

Chocolate and Cinnamon Cherry Cake

Preheat oven to 350°F (180°C).

Beat the eggs, vanilla sugar, and half of the superfine sugar together in a mixing bowl until frothy.

Add the other half of the sugar, the sunflower oil, cocoa powder, and flour. Mix in the baking powder and chocolate until well blended then add the sour cherries and cinnamon.

Use butter and extra flour in a round cake pan and pour in the cake mixture.

Bake for around 60 minutes or until cooked.

4 free-range eggs

heaped tablespoon (15g) vanilla sugar

¾ cup (150g) superfine sugar

⅔ cup (150ml) sunflower oil

4 tablespoons cocoa powder

2 cups (300g) all-purpose flour, plus 2 tablespoons extra

1½ tablespoons (15g) baking powder

3½oz (100g) chocolate chips

1lb (500g) sour cherries, drained

1 teaspoon cinnamon

1 tablespoon butter

A great combination of ingredients and very simple to make—very decadent.

Pochierte Feigen in Schokoladensosse

SERVES 6

Dark Chocolate *with* Port Wine Poached Figs

7oz (200g) dark chocolate
1¾ cups (425ml) custard
6–8 fresh figs
¾ cup (200ml) port wine
½ cup (100g) superfine sugar
white chocolate, to serve

Place serving glasses or ramekins in the freezer to chill.

Melt the chocolate by placing in a heatproof bowl set over a saucepan of gently simmering water. Stir gently until the chocolate has melted, this will take about three minutes or so. Remove from the heat.

Pour a third of the custard into the melted chocolate and mix gently until the chocolate mixture thickens; be careful not to over mix. Pour in the remaining custard and stir; the mixture will thicken as it cools.

Spoon the mixture into the chilled serving ramekins or glasses and put them back into the freezer to further chill until set, usually 20 to 30 minutes or so.

To prepare the poached figs, wash and quarter the figs and put them in a saucepan with the port wine and sugar. Gently bring to a simmer over low heat until thickened.

Cool then divide among the chilled glasses and grate white chocolate over the top. Serve chilled.

This cake is well known in East Germany and can only be bought in Freiberg and surrounds. As the legend goes, it was originally a cheesecake but there was no more curd left in the area, as the townspeople had used it to build the city wall, so they baked it without, creating the Freiberger Eierschecke.

FREIBERGER EIERSCHECKE

SERVES 4

Freiberger Cheesecake

DOUGH

3½ cups (500g) flour

¾ cup (150g) sugar

5½ tablespoons (80g) margarine

1 pinch salt

pinch lemon zest

3 teaspoons (10g) dry active yeast

1 teaspoon vanilla sugar

1 cup (250ml) lukewarm milk

FILLING

⅔ cup (150g) egg yolk
   (about six eggs)

¾ cup (150g) superfine sugar

10 tablespoons (150g) softened
   butter

handful of raisins, for sprinkling

flaked almonds for sprinkling

First, prepare the dough. Place the flour in a bowl. Spread the edge of the bowl with the sugar, margarine, salt, and zest. Whisk the yeast, vanilla sugar, and half of the lukewarm milk together; then pour into the well in the center of the bowl. Stir, adding more flour or the rest of the milk if necessary, until you have a firm dough. Dust dough with flour, then cover and set aside in a warm place for about 20 minutes. Knead all ingredients together and put it back in the warm place. After about 45 minutes, knead again and roll out onto a greased baking sheet. Prick several times with a fork, cover, and allow to rise for 15 minutes.

Preheat the oven to 325°F (160°C).

For the filling, beat the egg yolk and sugar until creamy. Add butter, bit by bit, and mix together to make a creamy mixture. Spread onto the yeast dough. Sprinkle with raisins and flaked almonds.

Bake for about 15 to 20 minutes.

These are very typical German Christmas cookies, but they are very popular to eat the whole year round.

Kokosmakronen

MAKES 30

Coconut Christmas Cookies

4 egg whites

1¼ cups (250g) sugar

¼lb (125g) dried, shredded coconut

3½ tablespoons (30g) all-purpose flour

2 teaspoons grated lemon zest (optional)

baking or edible wafers (½in/4cm in diameter)

½lb (250g) chocolate, melted, for decoration (optional)

Prepare a water bath by heating water in a shallow baking pan. In a bowl, mix egg whites and sugar. Place the bowl in the hot water bath and beat the eggs and sugar until the sugar dissolves.

Mix in the coconut flakes. Heat the coconut mixture to a temperature of 158°F (70°C), stirring frequently.

Remove from the water bath, add the flour, and mix again. If you like, you can add the lemon zest to this mixture. Let cool to room temperature. Preheat oven to 325°F (160°C). Place baking wafers on a baking tray.

Using a pastry bag with large tip, place little dough dollops on the wafers. Leave a little rim, because the cookies will flatten slightly while baking. Bake for 10 minutes then open the oven a little bit and bake for a further 5 minutes. The cookies should remain light in color and just slightly browned.

If you would like, you can decorate the cookies with melted chocolate. Break the chocolate up into small pieces and place in a bowl over the water bath. Stir until it has just melted. Take the bowl out of water bath. Dip the cookies into the chocolate to coat the top.

Note: These cookies are baked on thin, edible baking wafers, known as *oblaten*. Edible baking wafers are a crisp, white wheat wafer, similar to communion wafers. Check your local specialty store. You could also try edible rice wafers instead (available from cake decorating stores) or just grease your baking tray before placing the cookie mixture on to the tray.

Acknowledgements

The recipes collected in this book are our family favorites. To me, German food means homestyle cooking, food cooked with love.

It is with love and heartfelt gratitude that I acknowledge my wife—contributor and supporter—in this book's creation. The love and encouragement from my three daughters is also much appreciated. A special thanks to Bella for all her hard work with typing the manuscript.

To my mother, who taught me to cook with heart and develop a passion for food. To Hans—you were an inspiration who led me to follow in your footsteps. Special mention and thanks to my father, whose appreciation of food is second to none. To Katya, our restaurant manager—thank you for your beautiful dessert recipes. Finally to all at my publishing house. Sincere thanks to you for giving me the opportunity to share my German kitchen with others.

Index of Recipes

Aioli (*Aioli*) 162

Bacon and Potato Gratin
  (*Kartoffelauflauf mit Speck*) 132

Beef Pot Roast Braised in Dark Lager Beer
  (*Rindfleisch Schmorbraten Geschmort
  in Dunkel Weiss Beir*) 70

Beef Rouladen (*Rinderrouladen*) 66

Braised Apple Red Cabbage (*Geschmorter
  Apfel-Rotkohl*) 128

Cabbage and Beet Soup (*Rote
  Bete Suppe mit Weisskohl*) 37

Caper Dressing (*Kapern-Dressing*) 156

Carrot, Parsnip, and Cabbage with Mustard
  Seeds (*Möhren-Pastinak-Kohl-Genüse mit
  Senfkörnern*) 127

Catherine's Special Salad Dressing
  (*Catherines Spezial Dressing*) 159

Chicken and Walnut Salad (*Huhn
  mit Walnuss-Salat*) 72

Chicken Breast and Creamy
  Mushroom Sauce (*Hähnchenbrust in
  Sahniger Pilzosse*) 75

Chicken Breast with Creamy Mustard and
  Sage Sauce (*Hähnchenbrust in
  Senf-Salbei-Sosse*) 7

Chicken Schnitzel (*Hähnchenschnitzel*) 65

Chicken Stroganoff

(*Hähnchen Stroganoff*) 78

Chocolate and Cinnamon Cherry Cake
  (*Schokoladen-Kirsch-Kuchen*) 177

Coconut Christmas Cookies
  (*Kokosmakronen*) 182

Cod in Mustard Sauce (*Kabeljau in
  Senfsosse*) 47

Cold Dog (*Kalter Hund*) 175

Cream of Spinach Soup
  (*Rahmspinatsuppe*) 17

Cucumber and Yogurt Soup with Pine
  Nuts (*Gurken-Joghurt-Suppe mit
  Pinienkerne*) 19

Cucumber Salad (*Gurkensalat*) 130

Curried Sweet Potato, Coriander, and
  Pumpkin Soup (*Kürbissuppe mit
  Koriander*) 20

Dark Chocolate with Port Wine Poached Figs
  (*Pochierte Feigen in Schokoladensosse*)
  178

Duck with Sauerkraut and Apple Stuffing
  (*Ente Gefüllt mit Sauerkraut und Apfel*)
  109

Egg Cakes with Bacon
  (*Eierpfannkuchen mit Speck*) 116

Eggs in Mustard Sauce
  (*Eier in Senfsosse*) 119

Fish Goulash (*Fischgulasch*) 50

Flounder with Hot Dill Mustard Sauce
(*Scholle mit Heisser Dillsenfsosse*) 58

Freiberger Cheesecake (*Freiberger
Eierschecke*) 180

Fresh Chive, Lemon, and Dijon Mustard
Dressing (*Schnittlauch-Zitronen-Senf-
Dressing*) 154

Fruit Pudding (*Fruchtpudding*) 168

German Barley Soup
(*Graupensuppe*) 25

German Minced Meat Casserole
(*Hackfleischauflauf*) 114

German Rouladen
(*Deutsche Rouladen*) 69

Goulash Soup (*Gulaschsuppe*) 22

Grandma's Chicken Soup
(*Oma's Hühnersuppe*) 32

Grandma's Paprika Pork Cutlets
(*Omas Paprika-Schweinekotelett*) 96

Grandma's Veal Stroganoff
(*Omas Kalbfleisch Stroganoff*) 103

Green Bean, Bacon, and Walnut Salad
(*Bohnen-Walnuss-Salat mit Speck*) 134

Ham and Green Pea Soup
(*Erbsen-Schinken-Suppe*) 27

Homemade Chicken Stock
(*Selbst Gemachte Hühnerbrühe*) 81

Honey Mustard Chicken
(*Honig-Senf-Hähnchen*) 83

Horseradish Dressing (*Meerettichsosse*) 161

Lamb Steaks with Fresh Apricot Sauce
(*Lammsteak in Aprikosensosse*) 111

Leek, Potato, and Thyme Soup (*Kartoffel-
lauch-suppe mit Thymian*) 114

Lentil, Bacon, and Bockwurst Soup
(*Linsensuppe mit Speck*) 30

Marinated Salmon Steaks in Red Wine
Vinegar (*Marinierte Lachssteaks in
Rotweinessig*) 48

Meat Loaf (*Falscher Hase*) 106

Mixed Herb Potatoes (*Kraüter-Kartoffeln*)
137

Mother's Coffee Cake
(*Mutti's Kaffeekuchen*) 173

Mulled Pork (*Eingelegtes
Schweinefleisch*) 89

Nuremberg Sausage and Lentil Braise
(*Geschmorte Nürnberger Würstchen
mit Linsen*) 113

Orange, Thyme, and Honey Chicken
(*Orangen-Honig-Hähnchenbrust*) 84

Oven-baked Trout with White Wine Vinegar
and Leeks (*Forelle Blau mit Porree*) 53

Pickled Herring with Potato and Tomato
Salad (*Rollmops mit Kartoffel-Tomaten-
Salat*) 42

Pork Chops with Mustard Sauce
(*Schweinekotelett in Senfsosse*) 91

Pork Fillet with Freshly Stewed Plums
(*Schweinsfilet mit Gedämpften Pflaumen*)
93

Pork Stew with Sauerkraut (*Schweinefleisch
mit Sauerkraut*) 99

Potato Rösti (*Kartoffepuffer*) 149

Red Wine Cake (*Rotweinkuchen*) 170

Sauerkraut and Meatball Soup (*Sauerkraut
und Fleischklöschen Suppe*) 35

Seared Fillet of Salmon with Potatoes
and Citrus Salad (*Lachsfilet mit*

Frühkartoffeln und Zitrusfruchtsalat) 45

Simmered Bacon, Sauerkraut, and Tomato
Chicken (Speck-Sauerkraut-Tomaten-
Hähnchen) 86

Slow-baked Brown Beans with Roasted
Bacon (Braune Bohnen mit
Knusprigem Schinken) 138

Smoked Salmon and Warm Potato Salad with
Lemon Dill Dressing (Geräucherter Lachs
und Warmer Kartoffelsalat mit Zitronen-
Dill-Dressing) 55

Spiced Yogurt Relish (Pikantes Joghurt
Relish) 142

Stuffed Peppers
(Gefüllte Paprikaschoten) 121

Tuna Fishcakes (Thunfisch Frikadellen) 40

Veal Rolls (Kalbsrouladen) 101

Veal Schnitzel (Kalbsschnitzel) 103

White Cabbage and Bacon Salad
(Weisskohlsalat mit Speck) 144

Winter Vegetables in White Wine
(Winterliches Gemüse in Weissweinsosse)
147

a note on measurements:
1 tablespoon equals 15ml
or 3 teaspoons
1 teaspoon equals 5ml
1 cup equals 250ml

First American edition published 2013 by
INTERLINK BOOKS
An imprint of Interlink Publishing Group, Inc.
46 Crosby Street
Northampton, Massachusetts 01060
www.interlinkbooks.com

ISBN 978-1-56656-950-7

Library of Congress Cataloging-in-Publication Data available

Designer: Tracy Loughlin
Editor: Kay Proos
Proofreader: Catherine Etteridge
Project editor: Jodi De Vantier
American edition editor: Leyla Moushabeck
Food Photography: Graeme Gillies
Food stylist: Bhavani Konings
Production director: Olga Dementiev
Front cover photo: Hiltrud Schulz
Cover design: Julian D. Ramirez

10 9 8 7 6 5 4 3 2 1

Printed and bound in China